HEaR

KIANA LIN

HEaR copyright ©2022 Kiana Lin.

All rights reserved. No part of this book may be used or reproduced in any manner whatsoever without the written permission of the author, save in the context of excerpts for reviews or education.

ISBN: 978-1-7363255-4-4

Written, edited, and produced by Kiana Lin.

Cover design by Kiana Lin, featuring Karina Guerra.

www.creativeinklin.com

*For those who have been my grandmothers, mothers, and aunties;
For those who would call me sister–
And for our daughters.*

CONTENTS

ACHING	7
WAKING	39
DREAMING	85
About the Author	141

ACHING

How many histories
Lost
Because we refused to pick up a pen,
Couldn't open our mouths?
Will you hear her
Now?

Is it a relief or a cruelty
That nothing belongs
Solely to you?
Your thoughts
Have been attributed
To those that came before,
Your emotions
Have been named and expressed
By others–
No matter their complexity.
We are wholly unoriginal
In our individuality,
And, yet, we are left to feel
So utterly alone.

Little words,
A subtle nudge,
Meaningless, really.
Even so—
Every inch of me straightens.
I stare, incredulous,
Eyebrows creeping upward,
Jaw slackening and tensing at once.
My spine stiffens,
My insides heat and writhe,
And, when it comes down to it:
I laugh.
And I can't seem to stop.
I hate it.
Compliance
That I have been bred and trained for—
And I obey,
Out of reflex
Instead of Grace or Love.
I'm left with a begrudging
Indifference,
A numbness simmering just below,
For now.

Words fail me again,
Cannot hold the breadth of it–
Myself, yet reduced.

The right words,
At the right time,
With the worst outcome.
You think of me
Without truly hearing,
Listening, understanding.

You break her stance
With careless words,
And still expect her
To stand with dignity,
To rise with pride and poise–
As if she needn't
Rely on the shattered
And bloody bones
You left to her.

You set the table,
Laid it out
For war,
Then asked why
I couldn't dine
In peace.

When everything is at your feet,
Do you yet desire more?
I cannot give from
Emptiness,
My spirit is not endless.
My heart is still,
The blood grows
Cold in my veins,
And, even so,
You steal the very
Breath from my lungs.
My life,
Draining
Beneath your notice.

You offer ultimatums
Packaged as *options*.

How cruel
To know another is hurting
And to tell them
That your comfort is worth
More than theirs.

Even feathers,
When weighed together,
Form a tangible heft
On aching shoulders.
How much more
The crush of two worlds
Upon one fragile, beaten back?

How much of love
Is wasted on possession?

Sometimes,
I feel more like my own pastime,
Than a real person.

That's a me that is gone,
A girl who cannot be
Reclaimed,
A woman who has died.
There is no knowing her now.

They say a thing is stronger,
More beautiful,
For having been broken.
But the little flecks left behind
Accumulate.
How much of my soul is scattered,
Forgotten shards
Sacrificed for the future–
Never given the chance to glimmer,
Edged and repaired in gold?

Not this time.
Not on the outside.

–But Did You Die?

Triumphant, once—
When did we decide
To be beaten instead?

Oh the lies we tell
To keep our lives
Just a little bit more
Lovely,
Just minutely less
Lonely.

I thought everything–
Thought I– was truly alright.
It was a falsehood

Told just to myself.
Justification for all
But no peace for me.

Some things
You let slip away.
They don't–can't–change,
So you stay quiet.
The seldom moments
Pass into obscurity
And you only remember
The discomfort,
Recall the facade,
When you are present.
Forced to watch and participate
Until it dissipates.

A beautiful, delicate thing,
Twisted to fit our own bitterness.
A softly spoken lie
To comfort our blistering tongues.

There is no calm,
For she lives in a tempest,
A hurricane of her own making.
Because she would iron the sea
When it's only nature
Is twisting, wrinkling freedom.

You begin to refuse every hand
That passes along your way,
And, when the end of the line is reached–
When there is only one option left–
You tear into that appendage with a vengeance
Born from all those fists you knew before.
Leaving bloodied the last chance
At health and redemption,
And you're left to wonder why
They let you slip through
Those fingers you left mangled.

So young. Even so,
She has learned to keep her soul
Constrained to herself.

Still so new to the world,
Yet
We couldn't conceive of
Kindness without expectation
Dangling
Just overhead.

−They Can't Even Tell That You're Pretty!

Of all the mistakes made,
With every poor decision,
Overthinking has played
The villainous role.
While the heart
Alone
Cannot be trusted,
The head is capable of inflicting
The worst pain.

Only I can kill my potential,
My future self,
Poised with the sharpest knife–
My own doubt.
I hesitate,
And cut myself the deepest.

How far would you go
To keep your heart to yourself,
Your soul held hostage?

Discomfort,
A spark of anger on the tongue.
Fear,
The tickle of a single tear
Down
An exposed throat.
Terror,
Numbness, trembling, and
Dark,
Pervading all.
Still,
She finds confidence
Again.

WAKING

Rise above, be more
For you, your own reasons—or
Betray your own self.

You're asking questions
That have already been answered,
Loudly.
In her silence,
She has said everything–
By the angle of her brows,
The turn of her lips,
And her eyes that are too bright.

A raised voice,
Frightened eyes–
All because you couldn't find
The right words
For loving her.

When is it my turn?
When do I get to rage
And scream and be
Unreasonable?
Just for the sake of it.
When do I get to live
Free of the fear of consequence?
It's not my lot,
You say?
Then tell me again
How your life is not one
Of privilege?

Stifled and trapped
Beneath bone
And blood
And flesh,
Caged within walls of muscle
And wrung out
Over and over.
It took a jolt, a smack, a shove–
To loose them from their prison.
But, finally,
The feelings leaked out
Until the words gushed
And, slowly, ran dry.
My insides burst forth
To be discovered and seen
And known.

Pain on stabbing pain,
Numbness setting in,
Only one thing remaining–
A single point of contention,
A prick of awareness.
The source never where it ought to be,
The undercurrent carrying more
Than you would know.
All that you see, just the illusion,
The truth so far from the light.

Is it more dangerous
To have words?
Or to abandon
What they represent?

The memories don't leave,
And–it's somehow worse
That the instincts stay–
The feelings linger
Until you almost wish they
Would finally abandon you
To the bliss of forgetfulness.

What ever happened to regret?
Not guilt or shame,
But the bone-deep,
Soul-twisting ache
Of wanting,
Knowing, it can never
Be yours in truth.

Are we so easily consoled?
Won over by the pretty,
Peddled to by the petty–
No striving.
Longing forgotten,
A zenith, ever out of reach.

Is there nothing worthwhile?
Worth the deprivation of sleep,
Fingers cramping,
Hope giving out,
Then,
Achieving–finally–
Something of meaning.

A choice, once forced,
Is lost forever.
You ask me to decide,
Giving only two options:
Your own best case
And my heart's demise.
So I choose.
I chose.

–Neither

I am a woman of glass–
Only in cooling off
Do I become hardened,
Do I risk becoming shattered.

I'm feeling brittle,
As I hold myself together
With leather and darkness.
The shadows linger,
So I dangle pink and gold–
Delicately enticing–
From ears and fingers.
I'm drowning inside,
But I smile too bright,
I laugh too often.
Tonight there isn't much to me,
Except cyclical contrasts
And banked tears.

My eyes are mostly brown,
Golden dirt on a good day.
But,
On the worst days,
They turn vibrant.
Green, green, green–
Sprouted and watered
By tears.

I am not okay.
I'm feeling so stupidly weak and useless.
This body of mine
Is not the one I remember,
And I'm not happy with it
And I'm feeling insecure
And like it will be impossible
To look, feel, move, and be appreciated
In the ways that I am used to.
And then I'm furious
For having those worthless thoughts,
For being so stereotypical and selfish,
For conforming to outside influence.
I take a breath, another, and know–
I'm not okay,
But I will be.

Never set in stone,
A new time moving forward–
A new you to come.

The world is changing,
Or is it just me, growing,
On this quest alone?

Is it truth to you?
You understand, and yet–
Are you confident in
The Knowing?

A gentle nudge
In the right direction.
A subtle and contrite spirit–
You are in need of love.

A punishing shove
Off the cliff of indecision.
A stubborn and direct soul–
You are in need of respect.

I can tell you what I see,
But you will still only hear
What you know and understand.
My life is not limited by my view,
But in your comprehension.

Such pride for my logic,
Excitement at my indignation.
Where is the joy in my quietude,
Celebration of my intuition?
Why are the only things
You acknowledge–
My struggles-turned-triumphs–
Those aspects you would try
To claim?

My resistance
Is not a rejection of you,
But your way of thinking
Is a dismissal of me–
Wholly, as I am.

I will not be subjected
To your verbal assaults
Packaged delicately in
Prettily worded lies.

Tell me, in your own words, about me,
About my feelings and my hurts.
Tell me my thoughts, if you know,
And then let me be Judge.
Do you like it now?
Ire offered–
Poisoned,
Sweet.

They say,
I would've been good for you.
There is no such thing.
You could be the best of humanity,
And, yet,
The only way to be good for someone–
If they allow it.

You don't own me, you say.
Darling,
Why did you ever let them
Think that they did?
It is difficult enough
To reclaim what is stolen—
Harder, still, to take back
What is freely given.

If you only acknowledge the
Limitations,
If you complain always about the
Control,
You jail yourself more surely–
Forfeit your freedoms in ways
That no one else ever could
Steal them from your fists.

Hair flowing, head tilted just so,
Fluttering lashes brushing her cheeks:
She conveys freedom, whimsy.
Yet, all I see–
The cage constructed,
Made of her own volition.
She hides her face, closes her eyes,
And imprisons her soul.

You live your life
Inhibited by the fact
That you are too afraid
To truly inhabit
Your own body.

Conceived with furtive eyes,
Grown via sharp elbows
And piercing giggles–
Kind words birthed in whispers.
Beautiful sentiments
Aborted before they reach
The necessary ears.

What is set for you?
You manage to seem the same
While taking the form of
A living, breathing tempest,
Whirling with indignation.
Is your only consistency
Your ability to change?

My tears, all for you
Because pain echoes deeply,
Seeps into my soul.

My voice is a world,
My throat is a home,
And it's raining inside.

I am a reclamation project
In progress,
Digging up and refurbishing
The pieces of myself
That have fallen
To disuse.

I have been the one
Little girls look up to,
Been the example and even
Fashioned as a standard,
Unattainable.
But I am now become the woman
Of their mother's cautionary tales.
Shouldn't I always have been?

I just met her,
I thought.
But I knew
That wasn't true.
I didn't know how,
Though I had always
Known her–
Since the sun and sky
Appeared.
It almost seemed
Inevitable.

How many of our
Curses
Are really just
Self-inflicted,
Self-perpetuated–
Could potentially be
Self-healing
Blessings?

I hate this place–
I've said as much,
Loudly and to anyone
Who could possibly
Hear my complaints.
But I'm done now.
Though the hate has
The overwhelming majority,
I won't give it voice.
Instead,
I will sing its praises,
Proclaim its opportunities,
Speak words of thanks
For its sheltering.
And, perhaps,
One day,
My heart will make room
To love it too.

I can only be picked up,
Propped up,
Pepped up,
And play pretend so many times.
Eventually, I need to make room–
Either I stand with help,
Or I must fall alone.

If you wish to gauge
The condition of your soul,
Look first to the state
Of your community.

Fighters, survivors–
Born and bred to rise.
No skulking shadows
Within this circle.

If only an inch–
Those that have
Supported me
Are those who have
Raised me.

So much more with you–
The definition of possibility.
In no way lesser without–
The birthing of capability.
Not for her sake,
But for yours

–Let Her Be.

What seems to you
To be drifting off
Is actually an awakening.
I am coming into my own,
Blinking my eyes open.

DREAMING

Your sentiments fly free,
But they will find no rest in me.

I am no longer a keeper of secrets.
I am no longer a bank teller
Tracking the lies and ordering the truths.
I am exposed and exposing all,
And I will not be responsible
For whether or not the information
Is dispensed to your liking.

Shaking so completely,
Vibrating apart:
Because the conflict
Of going against one I love
Is more than my body
Can comprehend.
Only my voice is unwavering.
Because my soul is safe–
Regardless of this fragile housing–
Secure in these truths that must
Be spoken.

You ask that I concede,
Acknowledge,
Even your missteps.
But I will not justify for you–
Will not excuse even these.

I sit here,
Serving you terrible news
With a side of dry eyes.
And I wonder
If you know—
To get to this point—
How many meals I had
That tasted solely of tears?

You want to see rough waters
To know something lies
Beneath the surface.
You think my calm eddies
Lack the depths you claim.
But your sharp edges
Show your hand,
While my dark currents
Are still to be explored.

There's darkness within.
Should I let it out? I bite,
Fangs–glistening, sharp.

–You Can Smile.

My experiences are mine
To wield.
They are not yours
To weaponize.

I am open to discussion,
But your mouth is closed.
I am willing to debate,
But you are the one with an unwilling mind.

Pretty much,
Kind of,
Sort of–
I am now doing my best
To rid myself of these terms.
Why dilute what I'm feeling,
Cut back on my thinking,
Just to make you more
Comfortable with
My reality?

Lower your voice,
You're so loud.
But I finally found my volume,
And I cannot–will not–
Be relegated to whispers now.

Speak—in your own words,
Tell me the meaning behind
All that I would say.

I listen, thinking—
You understand only words
You shape with *your* tongue.

My will is my legacy,
Your cowardice is your mortality–
Cross me at your own peril.

The cages I built
Of fear and sluggishness,
Of *maybe*'s and *yesterday*'s–

I don't want them anymore.

Quiet the harsh thoughts,
Throw out the complacency:
Give me back my vibrancy.

What shifted,
From one moment
To the next?
Are your circumstances
Really so different?
Are you a slight breeze,
Blown about in any–
In every–direction?
Or are you the tidal wave
Bending nature
To your will?

All the speculation, all the hints,
And what did it get you?
Her mind is a palace,
A world unto her own.
A sprawling orchard, blooming–
Only in her own time.

You ask me about the leaves,
But I'm busy pouring into my roots.

What you call me is unimportant.
I am so much more than your words,
A living soul beneath your
Perceptions. Even a
Single name cannot,
Nor will ever,
Possibly
Contain
Me.

The things that hurt us the worst,
Do their best to shape us.

There is work unknown,
Actions that go unexplained,
Growth they never see.

No space for anger,
No room for hurt–
The only availability
Is for building tomorrow.

She is not your battleground.

We are not the victims,
Life did not happen to us,
That time does not define our being.
No, we are not the victims:
We are the survivors–
We are the victors.

There is a time to stand,
To raise a fist,
To sound the battle cry.
But now is a time
For a strong mien,
A display of poise–
Grace and cunning in repose.

When given a choice,
Be more than the expected–
Be what is needed.

As flames do not merely burn,
You are more.
Hidden within you is your purpose–
Find it.

Hopes born of dreams
Can only be inferior to
Dreams forged in purpose.

A heart can be drained,
A mind is easily broken,
But not so the soul.
We are creatures of Spirit,
Ever replenishing,
And evergreen.

She isn't sunshine or rainbows,
She isn't gentle waves,
Or even a quiet rain.
She is a hurricane–
In every sense.

She should come with a warning label,
Probably.
Definitely.
But I would not have her apologize for a
Single
Moment
Of her incredible, rare, brilliance.

She is a presence,
A whirl of momentum
That sweeps along
On her own path.
She is ever-changing and growing.
A lightning strike
Of emotion
And the rumbling thunder
Lingering to show
Which way
The unpredictable winds will go.
She is no dark, oppressive cloud,
But a force of nature
To cleanse and bring
The pounding rush
Of blood
And palpable excitement.
She is like a storm
And the calm that follows,
All rolled up in one.

She is striking,
Cold and sharp and painful
To face.
She is beautiful,
Healing warmth and welcoming,
Smooth and soothing.
She is pretty
In a tingly, nerve-wracking
Sort of way.
She is stunning,
Serene and lulling
In her manner.
And you,
Would you only
Notice her features and form?

Is this *your* body?
Has it been with you since your beginning?
Has it given you
Every moment since creation?
Then who are you
To name its weaknesses and strengths?
None but its master may determine
Whether or not the service is
Satisfactory, praiseworthy.
And of my own form,
I am the queen,
Who has been sheltered and harbored well.
I seek no speedy escape
From within this palace
Of ivory and crimson and gold.

I have no waif's figure.
I was made to look
Well-fed and capable.
I was made to look
Well-used to laughter.
I was made to look,
Well–like love.

Don't love me
Simply to fill the silence.
Do not love me
Because it is convenient.
Love me
Because there are no other words–
Love me
Because what else could you do?

You cannot simply
Fall in love with the sky
In one night.

You notice whole constellations
Until singular stars always draw–
And capture–your attention.

You grow to enjoy the view
With every cloud
And through each storm.

If it is developed in one day,
Based on one glance,
It is not love.

I am loud thoughts
And quiet words.
Warm and dappled, winding trails
And cold, snapping branches.
I am death descending and life rising.
The eternal turn,
The endless cycle–
Fixed and yet still changing,
Impossible and continuing.
I am shifting purples, deepening blues,
Flaming, burning orange,
And charred, blackest dark.
I am shrieking wind
And I am whispering leaves.
I am a mountain, a forest, a raging river,
A season, and a universe–
The ever expanding,
Contained.

Know me never,
Learn me always.

She is filling out,
Learning the shape and the feel
Of her stretching soul.

Wisdom, since ancient times,
Is so often depicted as
A woman–of course.
What else could she be?

Harsh in her delicacies,
Sharp as she wilts,
Moving in death,
And beautiful as she decays.

Unbridled life,
Implacable death,
My body a vessel–
At once–of both.
Each ever present,
Never winning,
Always losing:
A marvel of balance.

I place my trust deep,
Buried in the ground
That it may grow and bloom,
Beyond even my dearest
Imaginings.

So much room to grow,
Much to test against her will,
Yet her spirit is up to the task.

Your spirit has always stretched
Beyond your fragile, mortal cage.
You have not yet learned
To shrink and bury your soul–
Locking it away in the darkness–
Hiding in the expectations of the world.

Asking for help is either
An act of great courage
Or
A sign of complete assurance,
And that spells all the difference–
Points out the discrepancies–
Of a community.

Anything you need.
And I mean it.
My normal boundaries
Don't apply to you,
Chosen few.
Because you never ask,
I will always offer
And jump when you
Finally say.

Obligation is not something
I carry on my back,
Weighing me down.
It is a gift I cradle,
My choice to hold
For my loved ones.

Just a loving hand
Upon a shaved and cold head–
Warmth and acceptance.

Let her see the tears
As they run down
The contours of your face.
Let her see the liquid–
That special form of bravery.

Our ability to feel–
To have a common,
Innate knowing–
It is a thing of beauty
In a world so divided.

The thoughts that you choose,
The way you arrange your mind–
It is beautiful.

Your reality–
No matter how mundane–
Is capable of exquisite
Magic.

As if in a dream,
The real world beckons her on,
And she bids it: *Wait*.

About the Author

HEaR is Kiana Lin's third published work, and she is–of course–still writing! To follow along on her journey and learn more, visit her website:

www.creativeinklin.com

Ever since she was a child, Kiana Lin has had a love of words. From her first made up phrase to fit her stubborn idea to learning to read out of a spiteful need for independence, she took in every bit of wordplay and storytelling craft that she could. Then, one summer, a creative writing assignment led to a late brainstorming session in her aunt's and uncle's kitchen. That one night sparked the desire to create something she would enjoy reading for herself.

And then she never stopped.

www.ingramcontent.com/pod-product-compliance
Lightning Source LLC
Chambersburg PA
CBHW070045120526
44589CB00035B/2324